There are several spices that help enhance our life immensely. Among those, Turmeric and Alum are regular items which we find around us, but most of us are unaware about their curative properties as they have numerous unexplored healing powers. In this book, you will find a cure for every big or small diseases and definitely will realise what treasure nature holds.

Improve Your Health

Price: Rs. 40/- Each

with the new series

By Dr. Rajeev Sharma

Vegetables

Fruits & Flowers

Honey

Spices

Apple, Guava & Mango

Carrot, Radish & Ginger

Dry Fruits & Medicinal Plants

Dairy Products & Juices

Lemon & Indian Hog Plum

Papaya & Bengal Quince

Wheatgrass & Grains

Garlic & Onion

Trees & Plants

Turmeric & Alum

Basil & Margosa

THE BOOK FACTORY

X-30, Okhla Industrial Area, Phase-II, New Delhi-110020,
Phone: 011-51611861, Fax: 011-51611866,
E-mail info@diamondpublication.com, Website: www.diamondpublication.com

Improve Your Health With
TURMERIC AND ALUM

Dr. Rajeev Sharma

ISBN : 81-288-0918-0

© Publisher

Publisher	:	**The Book Factory**
		231, Sector-15A
		Noida (U.P.)
Phone	:	011-41611861
Fax	:	011-41611866
E-mail	:	sales@diamondpublication.com
Website	:	www.dpb.in
Distributed by	:	India Book Distributors (Bombay) ltd.
		New Majestic Shopping Centre,
		Basement 2, 19 & 20,
		Sir Jaggannath Shankar Seth Marg,
		Girgaum, Mumbai-400 004
		Ph.: 23829508, 23879421
		E-mail : fhead@vsnl.net
Edition	:	2006
Price	:	Rs. 50/-
Printed by	:	Adarsh Printers, Shahdara, Delhi-110032

Improve Your Health With Turmeric and Alum Rs. 50/-
By: Rajeev Sharma

PREFACE

Ayurveda is an ancient age old science which has helped human beings a lot. In different ayurvedic texts, several home remedies are described with their medicinal properties.

There are several fruits such as apple, pomegranate, banana; vegetables like onion, garlic, radish, carrot, ginger; cereals; plants; honey; dairy products; water; wheatgrass; spices that help enhance our life immensely. These are regular items which we find around us but most of us are unaware about the properties of these nutritional substances. Balanced and healthy food itself is the key to good health.

The main aim of this series is to make general readers aware of these helpful healthy items, to which most of us are ignorant.

I have included those properties of each substance which are scientifically proved and are prevalent in our families through the times of our forefathers. Hopefully, you will find this series beneficial for the whole family. You can choose any one of these books depicting your choice and follow one formula only, at a time. If there is any need, you can consult an ayurvedic physician or can write to me.

Dr. Rajeev Sharma,
AAROGYA JYOTI®
320-322, Teachers Colony,
Bulandshahr (U.P.) - 203001
Email-sharmarajeev108@rediffmail.com,
doctorrajeev108@indiatimes.com

CONTENTS

1. Turmeric: General Information 9
2. Curative Properties of turmeric 11
3. Curative Properties of Alum 21
4. Spirulina: A Nutritious Alga 30
5. Soya Preparations 33
6. A potent Prophy Lactic And Medicinal Substance – Chlorophyll 40
7. Wheatgrass: Growing And Dosage 46
8. Balancing The Doshas By Food 57
9. Your Health: Guidelines From Ayurveda 60
10. Plant Foods And Their Nutritive Values 71
11. Herbal Tips 83
12. Immune System And Essiac 104

TURMERIC: GENERAL INFORMATION

Botanical: Curcuma longa (LINN.)
Family: N.O. Zingiberaceae
Synonyms: Curcuma. Curcuma rotunda (LINN.). Amomum curcuma (Jacq.).
Part Used: Dried rhizome.
Habitat: Southern Asia. Cultivated in China, Bengal and Java.
Description: A perennial plant with roots or tubers oblong, palmate, and deep orange inside; root-leaves about 2 feet long, lanceolate, long, petioled, tapering at each end, smooth, of a uniform green; petioles sheathing spike, erect, central, oblong, green; flowers dull yellow, three or five together surrounded by bracteolae. It is propagated by cutting from the root, which when dry is in curved cylindrical or oblong tubers 2 or 3 inches in length, and an inch in diameter, pointed or tapering at one end, yellowish externally, with transverse, parallel rings internally

deep orange or reddish brown, marked with shining points, dense, solid, short, granular fracture, forming a lemon yellow powder. It has a peculiar fragrant odour and a bitter, slightly acrid taste, like ginger. It provides warmth to the mouth and produces yellow saliva. It yields its properties to water or alcohol.

Constituents: An acrid, volatile oil, brown colouring matter, gum, starch, chloride of calcium, woody fibre and a yellowish colouring matter named curcumin; this is obtained by digesting turmeric in boiling alcohol, filtering and evaporating the solution to dryness, the residue being digested in ether, filtered and evaporated.

Medicinal Action and Uses

Turmeric is a mild aromatic stimulant seldom used in medicine except as a colouring. It was once a cure for jaundice. Its main use is in the manufacturing of curry powders. It is also used as an adulterant of mustard and a substitute for it and forms one of the ingredients of many cattle condiments. Tincture of turmeric is used as a colouring agent, but the odour is fugitive. It dyes a rich yellow. Turmeric paper is prepared by soaking unglazed white paper in the tincture and then drying. Used as a test for alkaloids and boric acid Bael.

•••

CURATIVE PROPERTIES OF TURMERIC

Turmeric is a stringent and sour in taste. It is a used as a beauty aid for a long time and a nourishing herb, which not only gives natural gloss, royal glow and luster, but also imparts vigour and youthful vitality to the entire body. Turmeric is thus a great tonic, aromatic, diuretic, expectorant, blood-purifier, skin-tonic, carminative, pain reliever, germicidal, anti-flatulent, producer and enhancer of red blood corpuscles, anti-phlegmatic, anti-bilious, protector of eyes, anti-inflammatory and imparts coolness to the system.

Bruises, sprain and wounds

(i) Applying the paste of turmeric powder with lime or water on the affected part-eliminates swelling and pain in bruises.

(ii) Taking 1 tsp turmeric powder with hot milk is also useful.

(iii) Filling the wound or cut, (from which blood is coming

out) with turmeric powder will stop bleeding and cure the wound/cut.

(iv) Applying the poultice made of gram flour, turmeric powder mixed with mustard or sesame oil on the sprained portion enhances blood circulation and provides relief.

(v) Tying a bandage of turmeric (prepared with 4 tsp flour, 2 tsp turmeric powder, 1 tsp pure ghee, ½ tsp sendha namak with water) on the bruised portion provides relief.

(vi) Giving fomentation with cloth soaked in hot water (500 lit. water boiled with 1 tsp sendha namak and 1 tsp turmeric powder) on the bruised part eliminates pain and swelling.

(vii) Giving fomentation with cloth (having one ground onion mixed with 1 tsp turmeric powder) heated with sesame oil on the bruised portion gives relief.

(viii) Applying turmeric powder heated in butter, oil on the wound and tying it with a bandage helps in quick healing of the wound.

(ix) Dusting turmeric powder on wounds also helps.

Skin-related problems

(i) *Ringworm white spots*: Applying the paste of turmeric rubbed on stone with water on the affected portion is useful.

(ii) *Skin eruptions* - Applying the paste of turmeric and sesame oil on the body prevents skin eruptions.

(iii) Applying the turmeric powder or paste on the body before bath, is a preventive against skin problems and also a depilatory substance.

(iv) *Urticaria:*
   (a) Taking -1 tsp turmeric powder with 1 tsp mishri or honey twice a day cures urticaria.
   (b) Taking halwa (made from 2 tsp flour, 1 tsp ghee, 1tsp turmeric, 2 tsp sugar, 1 cup water) in the morning cures utricaria.

(v) Taking roasted turmeric with gud cures itching.

(vi) Eczema: sucking tablet of ground turmeric with honey for 10-15 days cures eczema.

(vii) Pustules: Placing cotton dipped in turmeric oil over pustules provides relief.

(viii) *Freckles, spots:*
   (a) Applying the turmeric rubbed on stone with water eliminates them.
   (b) Massaging the face with Ubtan, (mix ground turmeric with milk of banyan & soak it overnight) an hour before bath eliminates freckles on the face and imparts natural glow.

Cough and Cold, Asthma

(i) Taking turmeric powder and little salt with hot water or sucking a small piece of turmeric or licking 1 tsp turmeric powder with ¼ tsp honey provides relief in cough and eliminates congestion of bronchi.

(ii) Taking ¼ tsp turmeric with hot milk is helpful in checking running nose.

(iii) Inhaling the smoke of burnt turmeric throws out the trapped phlegm.

(iv) Taking ¼ tsp powder of turmeric (roasted in hot sand & then ground) with hot water cures breathing problem.

(v) Taking turmeric boiled in milk and sweetened with Jaggery is very useful in cold and Asthma.

(vi) Sucking a piece of turmeric (like lemon drops) or keeping it in mouth at night cures chronic cold.

(vii) Licking tablets (made by mixing turmeric powder, barley powder and banasa-ash in equal proportion and honey) 4-5 times a day eliminates trapped phlegm in the body.

(viii) Massaging the throat and chest with little turmeric powder, ground black pepper mixed with ghee cures irritation in bronchial chords.

- (ix) Giving a pinch of turmeric powder with milk to children provides quick relief.
- (x) Inhaling smoke of cow dung cake with turmeric sprinkled on it, releases the trapped phlegm.
- (xi) Taking ¼ tsp of turmeric powder with 3-4 gulps of warm water acts as a preventive against attack of asthma.

Whooping cough

- (i) Taking 1 tsp ground roasted turmeric powder with two spoons of honey 3 or 4 times a day provides relief in cough.
- (ii) Taking betel leaf with little turmeric piece in it is also useful.

Indigestion & stomach problems

- (i) Taking turmeric powder and salt in equal quantity with warm water provides instant relief in acidity.
- (ii) Taking 1 tsp churna (grind turmeric 4 gms, sonth 4 gms, black pepper 2 gms and ilaichi 2 gms) after meal helps in digestion, eliminates wind and stomach ailments.
- (iii) Taking curd or whey with turmeric powder after lunch cures digestive problems.

Sore-Throat

Licking turmeric powder mixed with honey twice or thrice a day cures soreness.

Tonsilitis

Fomentation with the paste made of 10 gms turmeric powder roasted in mustard oil and then, tied around the neck provides relief to tonsils.

Blisters in mouth

Gargling with a glass of water in which a little turmeric powder is mixed cures blisters.

Urinary Troubles

Taking the paste of ground or juice of raw turmeric and honey with goat's milk (if available) twice a day, cures all urinary problems.

Small-pox

(i) Taking 1 tsp powder of turmeric and tamarind for 4-5 days acts as a preventive against small-pox.

(ii) Applying a thin layer of the ubtan (turmeric powder, foam of fresh milk and wheat flour mixed with mustard oil or fresh cream) on the affected part twice a day flattens the deep spots of small-pox and makes the skin soft.

Worms

Licking the paste (made of -¼ tsp turmeric powder and ½

tsp vayavidang churna with 1 tsp of honey) for 7-8 days heals worms and throws them out.

Pregnancy and postnatal care

(i) Taking 5-10 gms of turmeric powder with water during menses is an anti-pregnancy dose for ladies.

(ii) Taking 1 tsp with hot milk in latter part of the 9th month of pregnancy helps to streamlines delivery.

(iii) Taking 1 tsp roasted turmeric powder with gud after delivery eliminates weakness and cures uterus swelling.

Pain in breasts

Applying the paste of turmeric rubbed on stone on the affected part eliminates pain.

Gout

Taking balls of turmeric (mix -½ kg roasted ground turmeric, one finely grated dried Coconut 1 kg jaggery, 200 gms cashew nuts or ground nuts and shape them into balls) daily in the morning with basil or lemon tea makes the joints supple and provides relief in pain and swelling.

Pain in Ribs

(i) Applying the paste of turmeric powder mixed in hot water on the aching ribs provides relief.

(ii) Massaging the ribs with turmeric oil.
(iii) Massaging the ribs with the paste of turmeric powder in milk of the Calotropis plant provides quick relief.

Jaundice and Liver problems

Taking 4-5 gms of turmeric powder mixed in a glass of whey twice a day activates the liver.

Diabetes

Taking 4-5 gms ground turmeric with water or honey twice a day is helpful in curing diabetes.

Leucorrhoea

(i) Taking turmeric powder with sugar twice a day for sometime cures leucorrhoea.
(ii) Washing the private parts with turmeric water (10 gms turmeric boiled In 100 gms water) is also useful. Along with it taking one batasha with 8-10 drops of milk of Banyan tree before sunrise for 7 days helps in early cure.

Debility in Males

Taking about 7-8 gms of raw ground turmeric and equal amount of honey with goat's milk cures debility in males.

Dental Problems

(i) Rinsing the mouth with turmeric water (boil 5 gms

turmeric powder, 2 cloves and 2 dried leaves of guava in 200 gms water) provides instant relief.
(ii) Applying and rubbing the teeth with the paste of turmeric powder, salt and mustard oil strengthens the gums.
(iii) Massaging the aching teeth with roasted ground turmeric eliminates pain and swelling.
(iv) Keeping a piece of roasted turmeric near the aching tooth and letting the saliva ooze out also helps to cure this.
(v) Filling the cavity in teeth with roasted ground turmeric powder provides relief from pain.
(vi) Applying the powder of burnt turmeric piece and bishop's weed on teeth and cleaning them makes the gums and teeth strong.

Ear troubles

Putting one or two drops of turmeric (by roasting 2 pieces of turmeric in mustard oil) in the ear, cleaning it with an ear bud cures ear-related problems.

Eye-related troubles

(i) Cloth dipped in the solution of turmeric powder and water is employed as an eye-shade.
(ii) Dropping turmeric water (1 tsp turmeric powder boiled in

500 gms water till 125 gms water is left. Cool and strain it through a fine cloth) in the eyes twice a day and putting the cotton soaked in water on the eyelids cures pain, redness, irritation and itching in the eyes.

(iii) Applying a heated paste of piece of turmeric rubbed on stone on eyelids also eliminates pain, swelling and eye-troubles.

(iv) A decoction of turmeric powder with water as a cooling lotion on the eyes is useful in conjunctivitis.

Poison of Insect-bite

Applying the mixture of turmeric powder and lime over the affected part nullifies the toxic effect.

Coryza

Inhalations of fumes of burning turmeric passed into the nostrils cures coryza.

•••

CURATIVE PROPERTIES OF ALUM

Coryza
Inhalations of fumes of burning alum passed into the nostrils cures coryza.

Cough and Cold, Asthma
(i) Taking alum powder and little salt with hot water or sucking a small piece of alum or licking 1 tsp alum powder with ¼ tsp honey provides relief in cough and eliminates congestion of bronchi.
(ii) Taking ¼ tsp alum with hot milk is helpful in checking running nose.
(iii) Inhaling the smoke of burnt alum throws out the trapped phlegm.
(iv) Taking ¼ tsp powder of alum (roasted in hot sand and then ground) with hot water cure breathing problems.
(v) Taking alum boiled in milk and sweetened with Jaggery is very useful in cold and asthma.

(vi) Sucking a piece of alum (like lemon drops) or keeping it in mouth at night cures chronic cold.

(vii) Licking tablets (made by mixing turmeric powder, barley powder and bansa-ash in equal proportion and honey and making small tablets) 4-5 times in a day eliminates trapped phlegm in the body.

(viii) Massaging the throat & chest with little alum powder, ground black pepper mixed with ghee cures irritation in bronchial chords.

(ix) Giving a pinch of alum powder with milk to children provides quick relief.

(x) Inhaling smoke of cow-dung cake with alum sprinkled on it releases the trapped phlegm.

(xi) Taking ¼ tsp of alum powder with 3-4 gulps of warm water acts as a preventive against attack of asthma.

Whooping cough

(i) Taking 1 tsp ground roasted turmeric powder with two spoons of honey 3 or 4 times a day provides relief in cough.

(ii) Taking betel leaf with little alum piece in it is also useful.

Indigestion and stomach problems

(i) Taking alum powder and salt in equal quantity with warm water provides instant relief in acidity.

(ii) Taking 1 tsp churna (grind alum 4 gms, sonth 4 gms, black pepper 2 gms and ilaichi 2 gms) after meal helps in digestion, eliminates wind and stomach ailments.

(iii) Taking curd or whey with turmeric powder after lunch cures digestive problems.

Sore Throat

Licking alum powder mixed with honey twice or thrice a day cures soreness.

Tonsilitis

Fomentation with the paste made of 10 gms turmeric powder roasted in mustard oil and then, tied around the neck provides relief to tonsils.

Blisters in mouth

Gargling with a glass water in which little turmeric powder is boiled, twice a day, cures blisters in mouth.

Urinary Troubles

Taking the paste of ground or juice of raw turmeric and honey with goat's milk (if available) twice a day, cures all urinary problems.

Small-pox

(i) Taking a tsp powder of alum and tamarind for 4-5 days acts as a preventive against small-pox.

(ii) Applying a thin layer of the ubtan (turmeric powder, foam of fresh milk and wheat flour mixed with mustard oil or fresh cream) on the affected part twice a day flattens the deep spots of small pox and makes the skin soft.

Worms

Licking the paste (made of -¼ tsp Alum powder and ½ tsp vayavidang churna with 1 tsp of honey) for 7-8 days heals worms and throws them out.

Pain in breasts

Applying the paste of alum rubbed on stone on the affected part eliminates pain.

Gout

Taking balls of turmeric (mix -½ kg. roasted ground turmeric, one finely grated dried coconut, 1 kg jaggery, 200 gms cashew nuts or ground nuts and make balls) daily in the morning with basil or lemon tea makes the joints supple and provides relief in pain and swelling.

Pain in Ribs

(i) Applying the paste of alum powder mixed in hot water on the aching ribs provides relief.

(ii) Massaging the ribs with alum oil.

(iii) Massaging the ribs with paste of alum powder in milk of the Calotropis plant provides quick relief.

Jaundice & Liver problems

Taking 4-5 gms of turmeric or alum powder mixed in a glass of whey twice a day activates the liver.

Diabetes

Taking 4-5 gms ground alum with water or honey twice a day is helpful in curing diabetes.

Leucorrhoea

(i) Taking alum powder with sugar twice a day for sometime cures this.

(ii) Washing the private parts with alum water (10 gms alum boiled In 100 gms water) is also useful. Along with it taking one Batasha with 8-10 drops of milk of Banyan tree before sunrise for 7 days helps in early cure.

Debility in Males

Taking about 7-8 gms of raw ground alum and equal amount of honey with goat's milk I cures debility in males.

Dental Problems

(i) Rinsing the mouth with alum water (boil 5 gms alum

powder, 2 cloves and 2 dried leaves of guava in 200 gms water) provides instant relief.

(ii) Applying and rubbing the teeth with paste of alum powder, salt and mustard oil strengthens the gums.

(iii) Massaging the aching teeth with roasted ground turmeric eliminates pain and swelling.

(iv) Keeping a piece of roasted alum near the aching tooth and letting the saliva ooze out also helps.

(v) Filling the cavity in teeth with roasted ground alum powder provides relief from pain.

(vi) Applying the powder of burnt alum piece and Asafoetida on teeth and cleaning them makes the gums and teeth strong.

Ear troubles

Putting one or two drops of oil (by roasting two pieces of alum in mustard oil) in the ear, cleaning it with an ear-bud cures ear-related problems.

Eye troubles

(i) Cloth dipped in the solution of alum powder and water is employed as an eye-shade.

(ii) Dropping alum water (1 tsp alum powder boiled in 500 gms water till 125 gms water is left. Cool and strain it

through a fine cloth) in the eyes twice a day and putting the cotton soaked in water on the eyelids relieves pain, redness, irritation and itching in the eyes.

(iii) Applying a heated paste of piece of alum rubbed on stone on eyelids also eliminates pain, swelling and eye-troubles.

(iv) A decoction of alum powder with water as a cooling lotion on the eyes Is useful in conjunctivitis.

Poison of Insect-bite

Applying the mixture of alum powder and lime over the affected part nullifies the toxic effect.

Bruises, sprain and wounds

(i) Applying the paste of alum powder with lime or water on the affected part eliminates swelling and pain in bruises.

(ii) Taking a tsp alum powder with hot milk is also useful.

(iii) Filling the wound or cut, (from which blood is coming out) with alum powder stops bleeding and helps in curing of the wound/cut.

(iv) Applying the poultice made of gram flour, alum powder mixed with mustard or sesame oil on the sprained portion enhances blood circulation and provides relief.

(v) Tying a bandage of alum (prepared with 4 tsp flour, 2 tsp

Alum powder, 1 tsp pure ghee, ½ tsp sendha namak with water) on the bruise provides relief.

(vi) Giving fomentation with cloth soaked in hot water (500 gms water boiled with 1 tsp sendha namak and 1 tsp Alum powder) on the bruised part eliminates pain and swelling.

(vii) Giving fomentation with a cloth (having one ground onion mixed with 1 tsp alum powder) heated with sesame oil on the bruised portion provides relief.

(viii) Applying the alum powder heated in butter/oil on the wound and tying it with a bandage helps in quick healing of the wound.

(ix) Dusting alum powder on wounds also helps.

Skin-problems

(i) *Ringworm white spots* - Applying the paste of alum rubbed on stone with water on the affected portion is useful.

(ii) *Skin eruptions* - Applying the paste of alum and sesame oil on the body prevents skin eruptions.

(iii) Applying the alum powder or paste on the body before bath, is a preventive against skin problems and also a depilatory.

(iv) *Urticaria-*
   (a) Taking 1 tsp alum powder with 1 tsp mishri or honey twice a day cures urticaria.

(v) Taking roasted alum with gud cures itching.
(vi) *Eczema-* Sucking tablet of turmeric with honey for 10-15 days cures eczema.
(vii) *Pustules-* Placing cotton dipped in alum oil over pustules provides relief.
(viii) *Freckles, spots-*
    (a) Applying the Alum rubbed on stone with water eliminates them,
    (b) Massaging the face with Ubtan (mix ground alum with milk of banyan & soak it overnight) an hour before bath eliminates freckles on the face and imparts natural glow.

•••

SPIRULINA: A NUTRITIOUS ALGA

Spirulina is a blue – green alga. It is a helical member of oscillatoriacae (cynophyceae), with very delicate transverse walls, and occurs both in fresh and marine water. It is an ancient food. It was reported by Leonard and Compere (1967) that algal cakes, sold at the market of Fort-Lamy, Chad Republique, Africa were mostly made of Spirulina platensis (Nordst). It was found abundantly in small saline lakes north of Lake Chad in East Africa. On chemical analysis, it was found to have a very high percentage of protein and was suggested that, this spirulina might be a promising food source. Malack and Kilham (1974) reported the rates of photosynthesis are exceptionally high in these lakes and that spirulina platensis is frequent in them.

This nutritious-medicinal tiny alga is now thought to provide singly a whole range of nutrients ranging from proteins to vitamins (including cynacobalamin) and minerals. Its protein content, the highest ever reported, ranges between

65-70% and is three times that of soya bean and five times more than meat. It has full range of vitamin B-complex and is an abundant source of vitamin B_{12} which is essential for combating anaemia. Spirulina is also a good source of beta-carotene, a precursor of vitamin A, having twenty times more carotene than carrots and has high amounts of iron, calcium, phosphorus and trace elements like potassium and magnesium.

Its medicinal values are numerous and actually it is boon to human health, combating protein malnutrition, anaemia and other diseases. The high beta-carotene content finds use in curing glucoma, cataract and night blindness. Improvement in haemoglobin levels and control of diabetes have been reported in developed countries following administration of two to five grams of spirulina per day.

It has also been used as a remedy for pancreatitis, cirrohosis and hepatitis and acts as prophylactic against cancer. The alga tablets are also given to increase lactation in nursing mothers and improve their health and immune system. Spirulina can reduce blood sugar and cholesterol level effectively.

It helps to control obesity by affecting levels of phenylalanine, an essential amino acid in the body, and thereby suppressing appetite levels. It also contains many polyunsaturated fatty acids which help to reduce cholesterol level in the body on long term basis (10 grams of plant introduce 13 mg of cholesterol in the blood and provide 36 calories of energy).

Cosmetics preparations of algae rich in vitamin E have been found to improve the skin. When applied on cuts/wounds they help in quick healing by promoting cell regeneration.

The alga is cultivated by allowing to boom in sunlight in a suitable pond containing alkaline water and harvested using some efficient technique involving membrane filters etc. The Central Food Technological Research Institute, Mysore is working on this product and it has been launched as a health food-cum-drug.

•••

SOYA PREPARATIONS

The soya bean is the seed of the leguminous soya bean plant. Soya foods have been a staple part of the Chinese diet for over 4000 years, but have only been widely consumed in the western countries since the 1960s. Soya foods include tofu, tempeh, textured vegetable proteins (chunks, mince etc), miso, soya sauces, soya oil and margarine, and soya dairy alternatives.

Soya is an excellent source of high-quality protein, is low in saturated fats and is free of cholesterol. Recent research has indicated soya has several beneficial effects on health in addition to its nutritional benefits. Soya beans contain high concentrations of several compounds that have demonstrated anti-carcinogenic activities. These include isoflavonoids, protease inhibitors and phytic acid. The low incidence of breast and colon cancer in China and Japan has been partially attributed to the high consumption of soya products. The low incidence of menopausal symptoms in Japanese women has also been attributed to high consumption of soya. Soya diets have also been shown to reduce levels of serum cholesterol.

Textured Vegetable Protein

Textured vegetable protein is basically defatted soya flour which has been processed and dried to give a substance with a sponge-like texture which may be flavoured to resemble meat. Soya beans are dehulled and their oil extracted before being ground into flour. This flour is then mixed with water to remove soluble carbohydrate and the residue is textured by either spinning or extrusion. Extrusion involves passing heated soya residue from a high pressure area to a reduced pressure area through a nozzle resulting in the soya protein expanding. The soya protein is then dehydrated and may be either cut into small chunks or ground into granules. Textured vegetable protein may be purchased either unflavoured or flavoured to resemble meat. It is prepared simply by mixing with water or stock and leaving to stand for a few minutes, after which it may be incorporated into recipes as a meat substitute. Soya protein is also incorporated into various vegetarian burgers, sausages, canned foods etc. Besides, being a good source of fibre and high quality protein, textured vegetable protein is fortified with vitamin-B_{12}.

Tofu

Tofu is soya bean curd made from coagulated soya milk. Soya beans are soaked, crushed and heated to produce soya milk to which a coagulating agent, such as calcium sulphate or calcium chloride is added. The resulting soya curd is then pressed to give tofu. Tofu is sometimes known as soya cheese, and is sold as blocks packaged in water. It can be bought as silken tofu, which is soft and creamy in texture, or as a denser, firmer version. The firmer kind may also be purchased, smoked or marinated. Tofu tends be fairly bland tasting and is best used in recipes where flavour is imparted by other ingredients. Firm tofu may be marinated, fried, stir-fried, deep-fried, sautéed, diced and added to salads or casseroles. Silken tofu can be used for dips, spreads, sauces and sweet dishes. Besides, having a high protein content, tofu also contains calcium, iron, and vitamins B_1, B_2 and B_3.

Tempeh

Tempeh is a fermented soya bean paste made by inoculating cooked soya beans with the mould Rhizopus oligosporous. This mould forms a mycelium holding the soya beans together and is responsible for the black specks in tempeh. Tempeh has a chewy texture and distinctive flavour and can be used as a meat substitute in recipes. It may be deep-fried, shallow-fried, baked or steamed.

Miso

Miso is a fermented condiment made from soya beans, grain (rice or barley), salt and water. Miso production involves steaming polished rice which is then inoculated with the fungus Aspergillus oryzae and left to ferment to give an end product called koji. Koji is then mixed with soya beans which have been heated and extruded to form strands, together with salt and water. This is then left to ferment in large vats. Miso varies widely in flavour, colour, texture and aroma. It is used to give flavour to soups, stews, casseroles, and sauces.

Soya Sauces

True soya sauce, called shoyu, is made by fermenting soya beans with cracked roasted wheat, salt and water. Tamari is similar, but slightly stronger and made without wheat (and so is gluten-free). Fermentation for shoyu and tamari takes about one year. Much of the soya sauce available in supermarkets is not true soya sauce, but is made by chemical hydrolysis from defatted soya flour, caramel colouring, and corn syrup without any fermentation process.

Soya Dairy Alternatives

Soya milk is an alternative to dairy milk and is widely available in supermarkets and health food stores. It is most commonly made by soaking soya beans in water which are then strained to remove the fibre. It can also be made from soya protein isolate or soya flour. Compared to full fat cow's milk, soya milk has a lower fat content, a lower proportion of saturated fat, and no cholesterol. It is low in carbohydrate and provides a good source of protein. Some brands may be fortified with calcium, vitamin-D_2, vitamin-B_{12} and vitamin-B_2. Soya milk provides an alternative to cow's milk for people with cow's milk protein and lactose intolerance. Cow's milk allergy is most common in infants, and specially formulated soya milks are available for babies. Other soya milks are not suitable as sole foods for young infants.

Previously, the media has linked soya milk with having a high aluminium content. However, the aluminium content of soya milk is generally lower than cow's milk, and falls well within acceptable limits dictated by the World Health Organisation. Aluminium in soya milk can be regarded as negligible. Certain infant formulas (both cow's milk and soya milk based) produced from concentrates have been reported as having high levels of aluminium and their suitability for infants has been questioned.

A number of different brands of soya milk may be purchased. These may be sweetened or unsweetened and vary in flavour. Market leaders are Provamel, Granose and Plamil. Some supermarkets also sell their own brands. In addition to soya milk, a range of flavoured soya desert and soya yoghurt products are also available.

Other Soya Products

Soya oil and margarine are widely used and are high in polyunsaturated fats and low in saturated fats. Other less easily available soya foods include soya sprouts, soya nuts (roasted and seasoned soya beans), natto (fermented soya beans made with a bacteria, Bacillus subtilis), yuba (the skin formed on heated soya milk), soya flakes, soya flour, and high protein soya isolates and concentrates.

Mycoprotein

Mycoprotein is a food made by continuous fermentation of the fungus, Fusarium gramineurum. The fungus is grown in a large fermentation tower to which oxygen, nitrogen, glucose, minerals, and vitamins are continually added. After harvesting, the fungus is heat treated to reduce its RNA content to World Health

Organisation recommended levels before being filtered and drained. The resulting sheet of fungal mycelia is mixed with egg albumen which acts as a binder. Flavouring and colouring may also be added. The mycoprotein is then textured to resemble meat, before being sliced, diced or shredded. Mycoprotein is a source of proteins, fibre, biotin, iron and zinc, and is low in saturated fat.

Mycoprotein has been developed by Rank Hovis McDougall, and is marketed under the name of Quorn by Marlow Foods Ltd (owned by Astra Zeneca).

Mycoprotein is potentially a very useful food item for vegetarians. Since, early 2000 the Quorn deli and ingredients ranges have been approved by the Vegetarian Society. However, at present, the ranges of ready meals, burgers, sausages, etc still use eggs from a non free range source.

Wheat Protein

Wheat protein is derived from wheat gluten. It is sometimes called Seitan. Gluten is extracted from wheat and then processed to resemble meat. Wheat protein is marketed under the name of Wheatpro by Lucas Ingredients of Bristol. It has a greater similarity to meat than textured vegetable protein or mycoprotein and is used as a meat substitute in a range of foods. It is available in some health food stores.

•••

A POTENT PROPHYLACTIC AND MEDICINAL SUBSTANCE– CHLOROPHYLL

Many leading dieticians consider wheat grass as a panacea on earth.

There are many nutritious and prophylactic ingredients contained in it. It contains all the minerals essential for our body. It also contains vitamin A -18,000 international units/ 100 g, vitamin C-100 mg /100 g, vitamin B, E, K and Laetrile-B, etc. Besides, it also contains carbohydrates, proteins and fat. Many cancer patients have been cured with Laetrile. However, the most vital ingredient of the wheat grass is chlorophyll. Chlorophyll is contained in a special type of cells called chloroplasts. Chloroplasts produce nutritious elements with the help of sunlight. It is therefore a research scientist Dr. Bursher calls it 'concentrated solar energy'. Infact, chlorophyll is a substance that is present in all green plants.

But, wheat grass is perhaps the best source for obtaining plenty of chlorophyll.

We all know that, human blood contains a substance called haemoglobin. Haemoglobin contains hemin. From the view point of chemical formation, there are a lot of similarities between hemin and chlorophyll. In both of them, the arrangement and the number of hydrogen, oxygen and nitrogen molecules are almost similar. There is only one little difference between the constitutions of hemin and chlorophyll. Magnesium is in the centre of chlorophyll molecules while in the centre of the hemin molecules, we find iron. Magnesium found in the protons of chlorophyll is essential and beneficial for about 30 enzymes of our body. In the light of this fact, Dr. Wigmore calls wheat grass –"green blood." Dr. Hans Miller calls wheat grass "natural protons producing blood".

The constitution of our blood is a bit alkaline. The proportion of hydrogen molecules (pH) in it is 7.4. Similarly, wheat grass is also alkaline and its pH too is 7.4 and, that's why wheat grass is quickly absorbed in the blood and is therefore beneficial to our body.

It is perfectly logical to surmise that, wheat grass should cure anaemia (a state of body in which the haemoglobin percentage drops) as the chemical formation of hemin found in human blood and chlorophyll is similar. Some experiments were conducted to verify the validity of such a surmise.

Dr. Kohlar carried out some experiments on rabbits, rats and guinea-pigs. He took a few guinea-pigs and divided them into two groups. To the first group, he gave normal diet without wheat grass. And to the second group he gave the wheat grass besides the normal diet. After some time, it was noticed that, growth and development were faster in case of that; second group taking the wheat grass. Their haemoglobin count had also shot up.

Dr. Hughes and Dr. Later carried out some experiments on rabbits. They took out some blood from their bodies in order to make them anaemic. The quantity of blood taken out was in such a quantity that their haemoglobin count would drop by about 40%. Then, the rabbits were divided into groups. The first group was given normal diet besides some chlorophyll mixed with oil, while the other group was given the normal diet mixed with oil alone (without mixing it with the chlorophyll). After about a fortnight, their blood test was carried out. Findings of the blood test revealed that, the anaemic condition of the rabbits of the first group had been cured while there wasn't any significant change in the condition of the rabbits of the second group. This experiment

reached a conclusion that, in case of those rabbits who had been given chlorophyll, it was transformed into hemin and consequently, they were cured of their anaemic condition.

Encouraged by the results of this experiment, many other physicians have successfully employed wheat grass therapy for curing many of their patients of anaemia. Dr. A.J. Pattack once tried wheat grass therapy on a group of 15 patients suffering from chronic hypochromic anaemia. Generally, such patients do not respond to conventional remedies. But, Dr. Pattack put those patients on a strictly vegetarian diet. Besides, he gave them chlorophyll through wheat grass and alfalfa juice. Within a few days, their condition began to improve dramatically. Their fatigue and breathlessness soon disappeared and they began to feel energetic. Their blood test report showed a dramatic improvement in their haemoglobin percentage.

Physicians like Dr. Miller, Dr. Burgey, Dr. Wigmore and others have admitted that, wheat grass juice is an effective remedy for anaemia. They also noticed that, along with wheat grass juice if the patient subsists only on the raw diet, the results are faster and better.

Chlorophyll is a potent germicidal substance. It destroys

certain types of germs that are responsible for spreading certain diseases and paralyses some others which are equally dangerous for us. Taking this quality of the wheat grass juice into account many physicians have tried this remedy on a number of ailments such as pyorrhea, skin diseases, brain haemorrhage, T. B., heart diseases, atherosclerosis, tropic ulcer, varicose veins, varicose ulcer, osteornylitis and inflammation of the intestines. Such cases of remedial success frequently appear in reputed medical 'journals and bulletins like American Journal of Medicine, American Journal of Surgery,' 'Archives of International Medicine', 'Journal of Physiology' etc.

Dr. Offer Crantz had tried chlorophyll on 79 patients who were suffering from such ulcers of colon and stomach which were not responding to any other treatment. Out of them, ulcers of 52 patients were cured in a period ranging from 2 to 6 weeks. Barium meal X-rays taken after the treatment confirmed their complete recovery. The remaining 27 patients (some of them had been chronic patients since a long time) were kept on, chlorophyll coupled with strict dieting. Out of them 20 patients obtained relief in a period ranging from 1 to 3 days and were cured completely in about 6 to 7 weeks. All these patients were

advised to continue to take some wheat grass juice even after they were cured completely.

Chlorophyll purifies blood, boosts up the functioning of heart and leaves a favourable effect on the blood vessels, intestines, lungs and kidneys. It is an excellent tonic as it enhances the basic transformation of nitrogen.

The most important aspect to be taken into consideration is the fact that chlorophyll is totally safe and has no side effects. According to Dr Smith, chlorophyll is in no way harmful to human beings. It can be taken in the form of a drink or can be injected in the body. Dr. Smith's report is published in the 1944 issue of the 'American Journal of Medicine'. (Remarks upon the history, chemistry, toxicity and anti-bacterial properties of water soluble chlorophyll as a therapeutic agent, Smith A. J. - American Journal of Medicine, 207: 649, 1944.)

Wheat grass contains active chlorophyll in abundance.

WHEATGRASS GROWING AND DOSAGE

Celebrated American dietician and grass-expert Dr. Urp Thomas spent 50 valuable years of his life studying different types of grass. In the course of his study, he examined a large variety of grass types. At the end of his deep and long research, he reached the conclusion that, "Among all types of grass, wheat grass is the best of all. It supplies human beings with all the necessary nutrients. Only a kg. of wheat grass can supply nourishment that can be obtained from 23 kg. of carefully selected vegetables. Wheat grass juice is a complete food in itself and anybody can subsist on it alone for the whole of his life."

Besides chlorophyll, wheat grass also contains many other nutritious substances. It contains almost all the minerals. Magnesium contained in it is helpful in activating about 30 enzymes in the body. It also contains almost all the vitamins, barring vitamin D and vitamin B. Fresh juice of wheat grass contains a much higher amount of vitamin C compared to the fresh juice of mosambi or orange. 100 gms. wheat grass contains 18,000 international units of vitamin- A. Vitamin E contained in it is beneficial for the heart, the blood-vessels and sexual efficiency. Many physicians consider vitamin %, (laetrile) contained in it to be an effective and the only remedy for curing cancer. It contains many enzymes and gastric juices which are beneficial to the digestive system in various ways. About 90 to 100 mg. chlorophyll can be obtained from 100 gms fresh wheat grass. Such chlorophyll is always active and of a high quality.

The chemical formation O'J'L' the wheat grass juice bears a close resemblance to the chemical formation of human blood. Both the liquids are alkaline. Both of them have the same pH. And, that is why, wheat grass juice is digested and absorbed quickly in the body. It mixes with the blood very soon and reaches out to every cell in the body.

It is a universally acknowledged fact that, among all grains, wheat is the best grain for human consumption. It can be grown anywhere and is therefore easily available. The information regarding other varieties of grass is not easily available and some

of the varieties of grass may contain substances harmful to human beings. But, the wheat grass is a familiar variety that is completely safe and contains no harmful substance. Wheat grass can be grown in any type of environment and during any season of the year.

Wheat grass contains a special property that enables it to paralyze toxic elements of the body or to eliminate them from the body.

1. Alfalfa contains some of the best medicinal properties, but it is difficult to grow it in the home as its roots spread deeper in the ground. Besides, after the sowing the seeds, alfalfa takes longer time before its grass is ready for consumption. Its taste is also comparatively pungent.
2. The taste of barley grass is bitter. Not only children, but even elders find it unpalatable to take it for a long time.
3. Paddy grass is generally very dry. Very little juice can be extracted from it.
4. Palak leaves contain minerals in abundance, but very little gastric juices. Some people develop diarrhoea after consuming it and therefore, they can't take it in a large quantity. Besides that, as it contains oxalates, people who

are suffering from gall-bladder stone can't take it.
5. Other green-leafy vegetables such as dill leaves and fenugreek leaves also contain many medicinal properties, but their taste is generally unpalatable. And secondly, they are not easily available round the year.

Thus, we can certainly state that, wheat grass juice is safe, harmless, palatable and full of beneficial properties.

TECHNIQUE FOR GROWING WHEATGRASS

Now, let us discuss the technique for growing wheatgrass:

Selecting a pot

For growing wheatgrass very big and deep pots are not required. Take seven pots measuring one square feet and having a depth of about three inches. Take only seven pots because after sowing, wheat grows to the desired height after 7 days. As a substitute of pots, we can also use wooden boxes, the lower half of earthen pots, baskets or big tins. If there is a compound or a backyard in the house, wheat can be sowed in small flower-beds or land basins.

Soil and manure

Very sticky soil is not desirable for growing wheat grass. Barring that, any other type of soil can be used for growing wheat grass. But, do not use the soil in which some chemical-fertilizer has been mixed. It is necessary to add some manure to the soil in order that the, wheat grass may grow well and may acquire some more nutritious elements. In villages, natural manure of cow dung etc is easily available, but in cities where it is not easily available we can buy packets of ready-made compost from the market and use it. But, chemical fertilizer should never be used.

Quality of wheat

For growing wheat grass a better quality of wheat with big grains should be preferred. Wheat grass grown out of big grains is always broad and full of juice. About 100 gms wheat should be sown at a time. This quantity of wheat gives us about 100 gms wheat grass, which in turn yields 4 to 6 oz. of wheat grass juice. This quantity of juice is sufficient per day for one patient.

Before sowing the wheat, they should be sprouted. For sprouting them, first soak them in water for about twelve hours. Then, wrap them in a wet thick cloth and tie them tightly for about another twelve to fourteen hours. As a result of this process, they are sprouted well and shoots appear on them.

This procedure of sprouting the wheat prior to sowing them is a useful one. If the wheat has been recently harvested or is rotten or has insects in it, it does not grow well. The procedure of sprouting reveals all such things before it is sown in the ground or in a pot. It also helps to anticipate the percentage of the wheat that would grow. While, if they are sowed without sprouting them, it is on the fourth or the fifth day that the picture about the result would be clear and sometimes, all the labour, soil, manure and other material may just be wasted. Besides that, the patient would not get the adequate quantity of the juice on the appointed day. After soaking them in water and keeping them tightly wrapped, if only 50% of the wheat appear sprouted, it would be easy to decide that double the quantity of wheat is required for sprouting and subsequent sowing. This would ensure an adequate yield in the required time schedule.

Technique for growing wheatgrass

Spread the sprouted wheat on the soil bed. Spread them in a such a way that the grains are close to one another and remain almost in touch with one another. Now, cover the grains with a thin layer of earth. Then, sprinkle some water on it. Remember, water has to be sprinkled only, not to be poured over it. Overdosage of water spoils them altogether. If the water

sprinkled on the wheat grass is not just ordinary water, but water treated with magnets it produces better results. Wheat grass not only grows very fast, but also contains a higher amount of nutritious elements. This has been proved and verified through several experiments.

Technique to treat water with magnets

Take a glass of water and a pair of powerful magnets (of about 2000 gauge each). Each magnet has two poles: North pole and South pole. Place the magnets on both the sides of the glass in such a way that the north pole remains one side and on the other remains the South pole. Put a lid on the glass and leave it in that position for about 12 to 15 hours, at the end of which the water is magnetised.

When the grass grows (Technique to treat water a bit high, give water with magnets) only once during 24 hours. But, during summer, it might be necessary to sprinkle water twice or thrice a day. For giving water to the plant, late afternoon or early evening is generally considered to be the right time.

See to it that the pots do not remain exposed to the sunlight for more than 3 to 4 hours during the daytime. When the sun is blazing in the afternoon, keep the pots under a shade.

Remember, only one pot per day has to be prepared. Do not

prepare all the seven pots at a time. Sow 100 gms wheat in a pot on the first day. Thereafter, sow 100 gms wheat in a pot everyday for the succeeding six days. On the eighth day, you'll find that the about 4 to 5 inches high wheatgrass is ready in the first pot. So, on the eighth day, from that pot, cut the grass, with a pair of scissors, as close to the bottom as possible. Extract juice from grass after washing it properly. Never pull out the grass from its very roots.

Do not allow wheatgrass to grow higher than 4 to 5 inches as the proportion of chlorophyll and other nutritious elements starts reducing from the leaves thereafter. Besides that, their softness also reduces and as a result of that less juice can be obtained from the grass.

After cutting the grass, the soil from the pot should be spread over to allow it to dry in the sunlight. The same soil can be used after about 4 or 5 days. But before reusing it, add some fresh earth and manure.

Care of the pots and the growing wheatgrass

It is necessary to protect the growing and fresh and tender wheat grass from insects, birds and rodents.

Use wooden racks to protect the wheatgrass from insects, birds and rodents. Place the pots on the shelves of a wood rack and then cover the rack with a wire network or meshes, so as to allow the plants to get adequate air and sunlight. Wrap the legs of the rack with cloth pieces: soaked in castor oil or keep them in small vessels filled with water so as to keep ants and other insects off the wooden rack.

It is likely that sometimes during summer, wheatgrass may not grow well due to heat. So, under such circumstances sow maize seeds instead of wheat and extract the juice of maize grass. Maize grass is only slightly inferior to the wheatgrass in quality and medicinal properties.

PROPER DOSAGE AND TIMINGS

In the beginning, restrict the intake of wheatgrass or its juice dosage. In an ordinary illness or for a common ailment 100 gms. wheat grass or 100 ml juice per day is an adequate dosage. But, those who are suffering from some serious or chronic disease should start with 25 to 50 ml per day and gradually raise the dosage so as to reach a quantity of 250 to 300 ml per day.

Even after the disease is cured, it is advisable to continue to take 50 ml juice everyday in order to maintain proper health. Any normal, healthy person can also take this quantity of the juice to maintain his good health and avoid illness.

If the dosage or intake is kept high from the beginning, then it is likely in some cases that the patient may -complain of nausea, vomiting sensation, cold, diarrhoea or fever or similar other troubles. So, keep the dosage or intake low in the beginning and raise it gradually. But, do not get panicky even if the above-listed complaints arise. Dilute the juice before taking it. And, if the complaints persist beyond two or three days, stop taking the wheat grass or its juice for a couple of days and resume it only after the complaints have subsided.

Proper timings for taking the juice

It is advisable to take the juice early in the morning on an empty stomach. After taking the wheatgrass or its juice, do not eat or drink anything for about half an hour. The juice gets absorbed in the intestines within half an hour after of taking it. Those who find it inconvenient to take it in the early morning, can take it at any time during the day when the stomach is empty. But, intake of wheatgrass juice should take in the morning only, and should chew the wheat grass at anyother convenient hour or at short convenient intervals during the day.

NATURAL RESISTANCE POWER

We, the Indians believe that, health would automatically remain normal and in case, there is any trouble we can always take drugs to cure any ailment. Most of us are apathetic to matters of health. Generally, we are indifferent and inactive about maintaining good health. We hardly ever give any serious thought to our health preservation needs. In modern times, ignorance about the health perhaps exceeds our ignorance on anyother subject.

In reality, ailments or sickness are not absolutely inevitable. If our natural resistance power is strong enough, no disease would dare to attack us. If we do not disrupt the process of natural resistance, it would see us hale and hearty till the end of our life. No germs of disease can affect a healthy man with powerful natural resistance.

•••

BALANCING THE DOSHAS BY FOOD

Lifestyle and diet play an important role in balancing doshas. Fortunately, essential oils can help create changes in lifestyle and can be added to the diet. This chapter is intended as a quick reference guide to assist in your day to day living.

Reducing Vata

General Information: Consume warm foods and drinks, oily foods, foods with predominately sweet, sour and salty tastes. Oil your body everyday with sesame and essential oils. It is best not to eat alone. Best colours for meditation are yellow, orange, red. Avoid dark colours. Best stones are jade, peridot. Best metal is gold. Avoid cold wind, dampness, excess travel, television, radio, movies, excess talking and thinking. Practice yoga that is calming and grounding. Exercise should be non-vigorous and non-exhaustive, such as tai chi, walking or swimming. Use bulk and tonic laxatives like flax seed and psyllium. Avoid dieting and fasting, dry foods, cold foods and drinks and foods having predominantly pungent, bitter or astringent tastes. Meal should be small, but frequent. It is important to go to bed before 10 p.m. If prone to insomnia take at night that are calming and soothing.

Reducing Pitta

General Information : Cool foods and drinks are best; foods with predominately sweet, bitter and astringent tastes. Avoid food with pungent, sour and salty tastes. Have flowers around the house. Bathe in moonlight. Take walks in the cool air. At night, massage your scalp with coconut oil. Competitive team sports, which promote cooperation are ideal; also activities like hiking which are vigorous and non ego-producing. The best stones, to be carried on the right side of the body, are sapphire, aquamarine, azurite. Take flower baths. Do regular liver flushes; take the juice of 1 lemon, 1 tbsp. olive oil, 1 small diced apple or other fruit, blend and drink instead of breakfast (Vata and Kapha may add ginger, garlic and cayenne). Follow diet and avoid restricted foods whenever possible. For meditation, use blue and green colours. Best metal to use on the body is silver. Avoid excessive sauna, hot tub or sunbathing.

Reducing Kapha

General Information: Fast once a week. Foods with pungent, bitter and astringent tastes are best. Avoid or reduce sweet, sour and salty foods. No breakfast before 10 a.m., take light meal in the evening. Best colors are yellow, brown and red. Best stones are yellow topaz, coral and diamond. Best metals to use on the body are copper or iron. Take regular baths and saunas to promote sweating.

•••

YOUR HEALTH: GUIDELINES FROM AYURVEDA

The fundamental principle of natural maintenance of good health was expressed by Vagbhatt as – "Hitbhuka, Mitbhuka, Ritbhuka". Hitbhuk: means take food which is nourishing for your health and do not eat merely for taste. Mitbhuk: means eat moderately (only that much which is essential for sustenance of the vitality and stamina of the body). Ritbhuk: means eat that which is earned and prepared by righteous means and also what is suitable in a particular season.

Broadly speaking, the above principles are not new to us. We all might have read or heard about these in one form or the other. But, how many people (including ourselves) really pay due attention to these? In view of the life-style adopted by most of us today and considering the growing pollution in the gross and the subtle environment, we ought to be more careful about healthy food. This series is bringing us the pearls of knowledge from Ayurveda - the science of leading a long, happy and healthful life. In the last issue, we had mentioned about the twelve categories of naturally nourishing food as described in the Charak Sanhita. Here, we look at these in detail to have some practical tips on what should we eat every day and how.

1. *Shuka Grain (Cereals):* Wheat, rice, barley, maize, millet, corn etc, are principal ingredients of Indian cooking. The cereals are natural sources of nourishment for human body. Carbohydrates are their major constituents. They also contain about 6 to 12 % proteins. The presence of minerals and vitamins are, however, nominal in the cereals; only vitamin B is found in greater quantity in their outer sheath. The shelf life of these cereals ranges between one to two years after harvesting. Sprouted cereals have more nutrition value and are richer in proteins and vitamins.

2. *Shami Grains (Pulses and Legumes):* This category of grains consist of grams and pulses, which are rich in proteins. Gram, green gram, kidney-bean seeds, red and yellow gram and lentil, black-gram, soyabean seeds, dry-peas, etc. fall in this category. These are the main source of proteins for vegetarians. The protein contents and mode of metabolism of these are healthier and more compatible with

the metabolic functioning of the human body as compared to those in the non-vegetarian foods (meat, chicken, eggs etc). Taking fresh sprouts of whole pulses and legumes in balanced quantities in breakfast and main meal are an excellent means of maintaining natural health.

3. *Kandamula (Tubers and Roots):* Potato, sweet tuber (sweet potato), carrot, beetroot, turnip, radish, etc. are members of this class and naturally healthy foods. They are rich in carbohydrates and are important sources of balanced calories in our bodies and activation of metabolism. These, if eaten in appropriate quantities, are good means of strength and energy in the body system. These could even be used as substitutes for varieties of cereal dishes.

4. *Phal (Fruits):* As we all know, vitamins, minerals, natural glucose and carbohydrates are present in substantial proportions in fresh fruits. Amalki, apple, bilva (wood-apple), banana, black-plum (rose-apple), dates, figs, grapes, guava, mango, orange, pomegranate, papaya, sweet-lime, etc. are easily available fruits in almost all parts of India. According to Ayurveda, these fruits also have medicinal properties. Fruits like apricot, cherry, pineapple, strawberry, etc. could also be used when available. Ayurveda emphasizes

that, fruits should be eaten in their specific season, and should be naturally ripe. Over-ripe or rotten fruits are harmful. Raw fruits would be difficult to digest and will not have the desired natural qualities. Care should be taken to avoid eating fruits preserved in cold storage and those ripened through the use of chemicals like carbide. These have severe negative effects; frequent use of such unnaturally ripened fruits might cause dreaded diseases like cancer.

5. *Shakas (Vegetables):* Fresh vegetables are important ingredients of a healthy food. They provide us with essential vitamins, minerals and compounds. Use of different types of green beans, bitter gourd, brinjal, cabbage, cauliflower, cucumber, green-gourd, lady's fingers, tomato, etc is very good for health. Different types of vegetables supplement each other in fulfilling the body's requirement of vitamins, minerals etc. Likewise, the use of fruits, specific vegetables should also be consumed only in the specific season of their natural growth.

6. *Harit (Green Leafy Vegetables):* Coriander-leafs, fenugreek-leafs, green peas, mint-leafs, radish-leafs, spinach, etc should be part of a healthy diet. Iron, calcium,

and other minerals and vitamin C and E etc. present in these green leafy vegetables or salads, are essential for our body's proper nourishment.

7. *Shuska Phal Va Tilahan (Dry Fruits and Oil Seeds):* Almond, cashew nut, chestnut, coconut, groundnut, peanut, pistachio, etc. are very rich in proteins. The oil inside these provide natural lubricants and fats necessary for the body's mechanical and other functions. The edible, oily-seeds of sesame, mustard, etc. also serve this purpose.

8. *Ikshu (Glucose rich substances):* Molasses, sugarcane, sugar, treacle, and other glucose rich substances fall in this category. These are often used to sweeten the drinks and eatables. These contain hundred percent carbohydrates, which are the major source of producing energy in the body.

9. *Ambu (Watery or juicy substances):* This category includes all edible substances that are rich in water-content. Fruits like watermelon, which contain about 90% water, are prominent in this category. Major part of our body system is filled with water. Fresh lemon squash, etc. and juice of watery fruits, if taken in balanced quantities, also supply us with other nourishing substances along with water.

10. *Goras (Milk-products):* Milk, curd, buttermilk, cheese, etc. fall in this group. Pure milk (esp. that of cow) and buttermilk are described as 'divine' food or best source of nourishment for sadhaks. Many people observe kalpa (long-term fasting) only with the intake of milk or buttermilk. Milk (especially, cow-milk) is said to be a whole food in itself. Curd is also nourishing food with several medicinal qualities, if taken fresh and in appropriate quantities in different seasons as per one's *prakrati* (level of tridosha). Fresh cheese and its products (if not fried) are wholesome sources of calories. Buttermilk (takra) is referred in Ayurveda as an important medicinal food. Condensed milk and milk powder might be easy to preserve and use, and may help in making delicious dishes, but these are harmful to health, particularly in the cozy life-style we have adopted and because of the chemical synthesis processes used in their preparation. Use of condensed milk and milk powder or dairy whiteners should therefore be avoided as far as possible.

11. *Sneha (Oils and Fats):* Butter, ghee (butter clarified by boiling and straining), edible oils and fatty substances, if taken in balanced amounts, are also part of a healthy diet. These are highly rich in calories. (On an average, about

nine calories are gained from one gm of any of these substances). These help in fulfilling the requirements of lubrication of body parts (especially, joints) and energy production in the body-system. They also generally contain vitamins A, D, E and K. However, excess use of these substances is harmful to both physical and mental health. Extra care should therefore be taken to keep the level of proportion of this category to the essential minimum in our daily meal.

12. *Krattana Va Yaugika (Cooked Food and Edible Compounds):* Ayurveda considers 'cooked food' as a separate class of food. All the categories described above are independent of each other and, as we know, most of the constituents of these could be consumed raw or sprouted. Cooking changes the natural properties of food ingredients. However, taking this class of food is important because proper cooking (esp. of cereals and pulses) makes the food easily digestible and many of the new edible compounds produced under this process would also be of vital use in the metabolic system and other body functions. Cooked food could consist of members of more than one of the above classes and help in giving new combined positive effects.

Deep fried food, varieties of spices and arbitrary combination of foods of non-compatible natural qualities are harmful to our health, according to Ayurveda. The use of pre-cooked food-ingredients and the so-called "fast foods" should be avoided, as it has very adverse effects on our body-system. Apart from lacking in nourishing value this type of 'modern' food is very likely to impair the normal functioning of our digestive system and cause harmful mutations due to the chemicals in the preservatives, the artificial and chemical flavors. Having looked at the different categories of edible foods described in Ayurveda, let us now see what the Ayurvedic Principles tell us about —- what, how much and when to eat? Why to eat and how to eat?

What to eat? – The principle of "Hitbhuk and Ritbhuk" conveys us that we should always eat properly earned, pure, seasonal and nourishing food. A balanced combination (depending upon the physical and mental labor required in one's daily routine) from the above-described categories of healthy foods would be best suited. For example, you may use wheat, barley, maize, and some pulses, curd, butter, groundnuts, oilseeds, etc, in appropriate quantities with larger amounts of green, leafy and other vegetables; some sprouts should always be part of your food. Don't eat over-cooked or deep fried food; use of spices, salts,

sugars and oily substances should be restricted to the essential minimum. Desist consuming toxic substances, stimulating and alcoholic drinks, and non-vegetarian foods.

How much to eat? – The answer lies in the principle of "Mitashi Syat". Meaning, eat moderately. Howsoever nourishing or healthy the food may be, it would cause harm if eaten in excess. So, be cautious about the quantity of your diet. Don't fill your stomach more than half its space, leave one-fourth for water and the remaining one-fourth for air. Those doing physical labor need more of proteins, carbohydrates and fats. But, those engaged in sedentary and mental work or meditation-devotion etc, should take lighter foods such as boiled vegetables, thin chapattis, milk, sweet fruits, etc.

When to eat? – As per the vedic routine, one should eat only twice a day after performing *agnihotra* (homam) in the morning and in the evening (before sunset). In today's circumstances, the best timings for the morning meal is between 8 a.m. to 12 noon and for the dinner sometime before 7 p.m. This way, the food is easily digested and keeps the body strong and energetic. Take meal in time and avoid taking food late in the night. One of the major causes of metabolic disorders and varieties of diseases caused thereby is that people keep watching

TV and take food very late in the night. Remember! It takes about 8 to 11 hours for proper natural digestion of food. Eat only when you feel hungry. Eating is a kind of agnihotra. The ahutis are made in agnihotra only when its fire is lit well.

Why to eat? – Take food to maintain and strengthen the health and vigour of your body. Healthy mind resides in a healthy body. The first principle of the "Yug Nirman Satsankalp" guided by Gurudev implies - "We shall regard our body as the temple of our soul and maintain its sanctity and health by observing self-restraint and punctuality in our routine". The purpose of food is to sustain healthy and harmonious functioning of the body system, the physical medium of our life, to enable us to perform our duties towards God and His creation. Food is not meant to satiate the greed of our tongue or stomach.

How to eat? – Take your food gracefully in a calm state of mind, paying full attention to eating; food should be chewed properly. Enough water should be taken before and after the meal. Water is like nectar for our vital functions. Drink at least a tumblerful of water before taking food. Don't drink more than half a glass of water while eating. Drink sufficient water after about an hour of taking the meal. This helps in proper digestion.

The type of food and mode of eating should also take into account the seasonal effects.

In view of these Ayurvedic observations, one should take light and easily digestible meal and firmly resist from lavish, heavy stuff. As a preventive measure, drinking water should be boiled and vegetables and salads, etc should also be washed in clean, boiled water. Ginger should be used in food preparation to make it easily digestible. Vegetables like green gourd, lady's finger are suitable, as these do not increase gastric problems; use of sprouts or pulses of green-gram and roasted or cooked maize is also beneficial.

Ayurvedic scriptures advise against the use of milk in the month of shravan (the second month of rainy season in India) and buttermilk in bhadon (the third month of rainy season in India); curd should be generally avoided during the entire season of monsoon. Viral fever, malaria, typhoid, jaundice, conjunctivitis, gastroenteritis and skin infections are quite common diseases (in India) during this season.

•••

PLANT FOODS AND THEIR NUTRITIVE VALUES

Plants that are used as food and are also of value as therapeutic or prophylactic medicine may be termed as nutriceuticals.

Food is needed as fuel (energy) and as raw material for growth and maintenance of the body.

There are three principal foods - proteins, fats and carbohydrates. All three can be used as fuel.

Protein and carbohydrate supply the almost same amount of energy i.e., 4 calories / grams. Fat provides-9.3 calories / grams. But whereas fat and carbohydrate can be freely consumed, a good deal of the protein in the diet must be conserved as building material.

In addition to the three basic components, essential substances that can not be synthesized in the body have to be supplied readymade i.e., vitamins (A, C, B-Complex-water soluble and D, K, E-fat soluble) and minerals (Copper, Zinc, Iron, Manganese, Magnesium, Calcium, Selenium).

A balanced diet constitutes all the above substances in the right proportions ie., proteins, fats ,vitamins and minerals.

Malnutrition which happens mostly in children arises due to inadequate imbalanced diet. Most of the children die as they do not get proper food and become victims of fatal infections of lungs, intestine, atrophy etc., even tuberculosis, a common curable disease among adults.

People who are quite unaware of the nutritive value of plants always opt for conventional sources to tackle the malnutrition problems. But, fruits and vegetables available in the market do not let any child/adult fall victim of deficiency diseases, if taken regularly.

Magnifera indica, Linn

Family : Anarcardiaceae
Name   : Hindi   - Aam
          Sanskrit - Aamra
          English - Mango

Description : A large evergreen tree 10-14ft high with a heavy dome shaped crown and a straight stout bole.

Distribution : Throughout India. It is cultivated in most parts of the Indian peninsula. It is common in sub-tropical Himalayas,

hills of western and eastern ghats and forests of central India, Orissa, Assam and Andaman Islands.

Parts used : Fruit, seeds, leaves and bark.

Properties : Ripe fruit laxative, diuretic, antihemorrhagic, refreshing, restorative, linthotropic, ophthalmic, astringent, anthelmintic and diarrhoea, antisyphilitic and tonic.

Forms of use: Mango kernel, juice of ripe mango, unripe small mango (about torch bulb size), pieces of unripe dried mango seed powder and boiled unripe mango etc.

Phytochemicals : Vitamin A, C, flavones, carotenes, glycosides, sterol, terpene, aromatic acids, essential oil, fatty acids and phenolics.

Minerals, Amino acids and Vitamins-contents of Mango fruit

1. Fluorine : 0.3-0.7 ppm dry edible material
2. Iodine : 0.53 ppm dry edible material
3. Calcium : 96 mg%
4. Magnessium : 27.1 mg%
5. Phosphate : 25.0 mg%
6. Ascorbic acid : 16.0 mg /100g
7. Phosphorus : 16.0mg/100g
8. Iron : 1.3 mg/100g

9. Carotene : 2743 ug/g (Vitamin A 2309-15589 1.4%)
10. Vitamin B_1 : 0.08 mg/g
11. Vitamin B_2 : 0.09 mg/g
12. Niacin : 0.90 mg/g
13. Methionine and Lysine (Amino acids)

Medicinal Uses

* It is a powerful nutritive fruit, containing most of all essential substances needed for our body.
* It contains vitamins and minerals along with important chemicals that keep our body fit and fine. So, it is a complete natural food.
* Its unripe fruit (of about torch bulb size) if used 6 pieces at a time per day for a week clears all stones from kidney. This should be repeated consecutively for 3 years in the mango season.
* A drink made from boiled unripe mango with salt is a wonderful remedy for heat stroke.
* Powdered mango seed when taken thrice a day cures diarrhoea and dysentery.
* Mango juice is a restorative tonic. It should be taken throughout the season to stay healthy.
* Dentifrice prepared from mango leaves keeps teeth healthy.

Ficus caric Linn

Family	:	Moraceae
Names	:	Bengali, Gujrati, Hindi, Marathi - anjir
Sanskrit	:	Anjir
English	:	Fig
Telugu	:	Anjuru
Tamil	:	Simaiyatti
Kannada	:	Anjura

Describtion : A bush or small tree with a cylindrical stem, it grows to a height about 13ft and has an abundance of latem producing ducts. The rich green leaves are scabrous with a pubescent lower surface; they are 3-5 lobed with a cordate base and are borne on a long petiole. The flowers are monoecious, being enclosed in a flashy receptacle known as syconium which changes from green to deep purple as it ripens.

Distribution : All over India.

Parts used : Leaves, root, fruit.

Phytochemicals : Sugars, protein, salts, vitamin A and B, Coumarins and furo-coumarins etc.

Properties : Pectoral belonging to the thorax; applied to therapeutic agents which have good effect in respiratory diseases, laxative, emollient, energy giving, anti-boil, nutritive, tonic.

Forms of use : Its main use is as an edible fruit having high nutritive value. It can be used as a decoction and poultice.

Medicinal Uses

* A fig is high in calories and is easy to digest and assimilate. The latex that oozes out of the freshly cut leaves contain chymase (a milky fluid with a coagulate action), lipase, amylase and protease. It also contains a diastasic enzyme which when applied over uncooked meat increased maturation process.
* It also has an analgesic effect against insect sting and bites.
* The leaves can be used in decoction form to condition hair.
* Decoction of the young branches is an excellent pectoral (for respiratory problems).
* Fig is a highly nutritious fruit. Since, it does not contain any fibre, persons recovering from illness are specially advised to take it. It is a wholesome food which is easily digested.
* It is also effective in removing stones in the kidney or the bladder and also helps in the removal of the obstruction of the liver and spleen in subacute cases.
* The fruit is also given as a cure for piles and gout.
* It is also beneficial in infantile liver, piles and diarrhoea.

* Above all, it is very useful in leucoderma treatment, patients are advised to take a good of fig thrice a day for a month and use juice of fresh leaves on the white spots twice or thrice in a day and bedtime. They can also use moistened leaves of chenopodium (*Bathu Ka Sag*) on the white spots.

Luffa a cutangula (Linn) Roxb.
Var, amara (Roxb) Clarke

Family	:	Cucurbitaceae		
Name	:	Hindi	-	Torai
		Sanskrit	-	Koshataki
		English	-	Ribbed gourd
		Bengali	-	Thinga
		Gujarati	-	Kadavighisodi
		Tamil	-	Peypirakam
		Telugu	-	Aelavibua
		Trade name	-	Kukarvela

Description : A climber, leaves 4 to 8 inches long, orbicular reniform, 5 lobed, flower yellow, stamens 3, strongly ribbed ovary. Fruit 6 to 12 inches long, clavate, oblong obtuse, smooth, longitudinally ribbed. Seed 1/4 to 1/3 inch ovoid-oblong, compressed, black, not winged.

Distribution : Cultivated throughout India.
Parts used : Fruit, seeds, root and leaves.
Properties : Nutritive, bitter, tonic, diuretic, demulcent, expectorant and hypoglycemic.
Phytochemicals : Amino acids-arginine, glycine, threonine, glutamic and leucine. Bitter substances-Cucurbitacins, terpenes and saponins, Vitamins and Minerals-Calcium (18mg), Phosphorus (0.5mg), Iron (33gms), Vitamin B2 (0.001mg), Niacin (0.01mg), Vitamin C (5mg), Carotene (2.6mg). Presence of fluorine, iodine is also reported.
Forms of use : As vegetable, decoction, juice.

Medicinal Uses

* It is a nutritive plant and used as vegetable.
* It is a better tonic and diuretic.
* Seeds are emetic and purgative.
* It is useful in the enlargement of spleen.
* Leaves are good substitute for ipecacuanaha in dysentery.
* The leaves or its juice are used as a dressing of sores, inflamed spleen, ringworm, piles, leprosy and bites of insects.
* Oil of seeds is effective in skin diseases.
* The root is laxative.

Withania somnifera (Linn.) Dunal

Family	:	Solanaceae	
Names	:	Hindi	- Asgandh
		Sanskrit	- Ashwagandha
		English	- Winter Cherry
		Bangali	- Aaskanda
		Gujarati	- Asoda
		Kannada	- Hirimaddina gadde
		Marathi	- Aaskandha
		Malayalam	- Ammukivann
		Trade name	- Nagauri asgandha

Description : A small under shrub upto 1.5 inches high stem and branches covered with minute star shaped hairs. Leaves upto 10cm long, ovate, hair-like branches. Flowers pale green, small about 1cm long, few flowers borne together in short auxiliary clusters. Fruit 6 mm diameter, globule, smooth red, enclosed in the inflated and membranous calyx.

Distribution : Found throughout India.

Properties : Nutritive, tonic, alterant, aphrodisiac and nervine sedative.

Phytochemicals : Alkaloids, amino acids, sterols and neutral compounds.

Forms of use : Powder, decoction, paste of root and leaves.

Medicinal Uses

* It enforces fresh energy and vigour in a system worn out owing to any constitutional disease like syphilis and in rheumatic fever.
* Powdered root is very useful with equal parts of ghee and honey for impotence and seminal debility.
* As nutrient and health restorative to the pregnant and old people, a decoction of the root is recommended.
* For glandular swelling fresh green root reduced to paste with heated water is applied on the affected parts.
* For improving sight, a mixture of this plant powder, liquorice powder and juice of embic myrobalans is recommended.
* Removes functional obstruction of body, promotes urination.
* The antibiotic and antibacterial activity of the roots as well as leaves has recently been confirmed.

Amaranthus paniculatus, Linn.

Family   :   Amaranthaceae
Names   :   Hindi   -   Asgandh

Description : It is a small, herbaceous annual, leaves alternate, abovate, dotted, upto one inch long, half inch broad, tip pointed. Flowers small, in auxiliary clusters. Fruits are above ovoid, compressed sac, opening transversely.

Distribution : Common in plains of India.

Chemical Compounds : This vegetable is highly nutritious packed as it is with proteins, carbohydrates, calcium, phosphorus, iron, Vitamin A 2500-11000 I.U. and Vitamin C 173 mg/100gms. Seeds contain saponin which is slightly toxic.

Parts used : Leaves, root and seeds.

Properties : Carminative, nutritive, antibiotic, emollient, demulcent, aphrodisiac, antirheumatic.

Forms of use : As vegetable, decoction, poultice, juice, mixed with lemon and honey.

Medicinal Uses

* One should take it regularly to get rid of Vitamins and mineral deficiency. This can serve as a natural protein, amino acids like leucine, lyaine, cysteine and methionine.
* Taken at any stage, chaulai is believed to be useful in curing vision defects, respiratory infections and recurrent colds.
* The juice extract mixed with honey is a wonderful remedy against bronchitis, asthma, emphyscma and tuberculosis.
* For infants, a teaspoon of the fresh juice with honey makes the baby healthy and strong. This also prevents constipation and eases the teething process.

- * The juice of the plant mixed with a teaspoon of lemon juice fight against bleeding caused by week gums, nose, lungs and even piles.
- * A decoction of the leaves or roots is given in 1/2 ounce in diarrhoea, leucorrhoea, menorrhagia and impotence. A poultice of the leaves with honey is applied over inflamed and painful parts.
- * The roots are given incolic gonorrhoea and eczema.
- * The seeds are cooling, demulcent and powerfully aphrodisiac, they are given in leucorrhoea and impotence.
- * The leaves are sweetish, expectorant, vulnerary, antipyretic, emmenagogue, emetic, stop suppurations, useful in biliousness, fleshy tumors, toothache, burning sensations, liver complaints, inflammations, decoction as gargle in stomatitis.
- * Externally it is used as an emollient poultice, as an application in ulcerated condition of throat and mouth, as a wash for ulcers and sores.

•••

HERBAL TIPS

Constipation

a. The best way to deal with constipation it to change food habits. Milk, boiled vegetables, fruits and their juices should be taken in large quantities, together with foods containing a lot of roughage & fibrous matters.
b. 10 gms of Senna leaves and 5 gms of aniseed should be boiled in a cup of water with sugar, then strained and drunk before retiring for the night.
c. Half litre of milk mixed with 50 gms of khand taken at night will provide relief.
d. Another remedy is to take 40 gms of Gulkand with milk everyday.
e. If these remedies fail to provide relief, 6 gms of the rind of harr should be finely powdered and mixed with a little lukewarm and salt be taken.
f. Take *bathu ka saag* during the season for getting rid of chronic constipation.

Toothache

a. A paste made of finely ground leaves of basil should be warmed a little and applied to the aching tooth.
b. Ginger ground into a paste with a pinch of salt also relieves toothache.
c. Applying the clove oil is also effective.
d. Brush your teeth with dried, powdered leaves of basil to strengthen gums and prevent pain & pyorrhoea.
e. Brush your teeth after each meal to keep away dental problems.
f. Avoid chewing tobacco, pan-masala and other similar items to avoid early decay.
g Wash and dry neem leaves; Grind them to a fine powder. Sprinkle this powder over the toothpaste before brushing your teeth. You will never have complaints of tooth decay or any mouth diseases.

(A) For Vigour

Onion juice	... 2 tsp
Honey	... 2 tsp
Ginger (Adrak) juice	... 1 tsp

To be taken twice, morning and evening for ten or fifteen days.

(B) For Vigour and strength

Onion juice	... 2 tsp
Honey	... 2 tsp
Desi-ghee	... 2 tsp
Egg yolk	... 1 tsp

Mix the above materials and heat it on stove, add Mishri and take once in the morning for 15 days.

Leucoderma or White Spot on Skin

(If it is senseless, it could be leprosy then do not use this prescription)

Take *Bathu ka sag* daily during the season in form of *Roti* or *Dal-sag* and use its juice over spots daily at least twice or thrice. Take Anjir regularly for a month.

For Malaria

Basil	... 10 leaves
Bhang	... 5 leaves
Kali-mirch	... 10-15 pieces

Grind the above mixture to a paste and make pea size pellets. Dry it in shade. Take two pellets thrice a day.

For Nausea

(a) Neembu-pani at the time of nausea will be helpful.

(b) Soft Kheera should be eaten gradually to get rid of nausea.

For Purifying Blood

Taking a Mundi (a plant) juice daily (one cup) purifies the blood.

For Angina and Ischaemic Heart Disease

1. Puskarmula
2. Arjun
3. Kut
4. Proshnaparini
5. Guggulu

Above plants are equally powdered and 10gms powder is left ovenight in a cup of water. Take it in the morning.

Fever/Headache/Bodyache/Malaria

1. *Ghiraita* ... 5 leaves
2. Neem leaves ... 5 leaves
3. Basil ... 10 leaves
4. Lemon Grass ... 5 leaves
5. Black pepper ... 10-15 pieces

Mix all, boil & strain, add sugar to taste. Take half cup thrice a day.

Dysentery/Tenusmus/Diarrhoea

(a) Grind whole plant of Duddhi in water. Strained water extract (half cup) if taken twice or thrice a day provides quick relief.

For cold

    Basil   ...   10 leaves
    Honey   ...   2 tsp

Make the paste of leaves and mix with honey. Taken in the morning, it will keep out cold & cough away and will also help in bringing down blood pressure.

Eczema

(a) Apply the garlic juice & lemon juice on the affected part. It will clear fungus infection.

(b) Eczema / Fungus infection of nails, hand & feet will be cleared with the use of Mehndi (Use continuously for a week). Avoid excess indulgence in water.

(c) Use of basil leaves and lemon juice to the infected part will also cure eczema.

High Blood pressure

(a) 1. Garlic   ... 5 cloves
    2. Basil   ... 5 leaves
    3. Honey   ... 4 tsp

Make a paste of above ingredients and eat it once in the morning without taking anything.

(b) Take two bananas daily to balance excess sodium in the body. Banana contains enough potassium to cut all effects of sodium (we use as common salt).

Stomach Upsets
1. Basil ... 5 leaves
2. Ginger (Adrak) ... Few pieces
3. Black Pepper ... 10-15 pieces

Boil these material. Strain and drink twice or thrice (half cup).

Cough
(a) Dip pieces of one medium size onion in 10 ml of pure honey, leave it overnight. Remove the pieces and take one spoon juice thrice a day.
 - Muli as vegetable
 - Anar & Angur juice
 - Liv-52 Tablet, 2 tablet thrice a day
 - Take rest.

Cuts/Wounds
(a) Sprinkle powdered Mehndi or
(b) Sprinkle powdered turmeric.

Arthritis/Gout
(a) Boil mustard oil (10 ml) with one moderate pack of Garlic bulb, apply on the affected parts 3/4 times a day.
(b) Massage with camphor oil 3/4 times a day on the affected parts.

(c) Apply the warm mustard oil on the affected parts at the time of bed rest and cover them with Dhatura leaves overnight. Keep doing it for 15 days. Repeat again as per need.

(d) Massage with Turpentine oil/Eucalyptus oil 3/4 times a day on the affected part. Cover that portion with a wet towel and gradually pour hot water (not very hot) from kettle on it. It provides a great relief.

For Body Resistance to Disease

A mixture of amla, harr, bahera and herb giloya (1:1:1:1) if taken regularly makes the person immune to illness.

To Stop Oozing Blood

Sprinkle turmeric powder, flowing of blood will be stopped.

Hoarse Voice

Sprinkle common salt on the small pieces of ginger (adrak). Take the pieces gradually one by one.

Eyebrow

Put a little warm castor oil on scanty eyebrows. This will enhance their growth.

Hair

(a) Extract the juice of the aloe-vera plant and rub it into your scalp. This ensures the healthy growth of hair.

(b) For glowing hair, grind a few whole green grams, lemon peels, a handful of curry leaves and a few "rithas" to a paste and apply to the hair before washing off.

Insect Bite

To cure an insect bite apply any balm on it. It will relieve you of the itchy sensation.

Kidneys

Dry basil seeds and grind them with an equal quantity of sugar. One spoon of this powder, taken every morning, is good for the kidney.

Sore Throat

Drink tea with a pinch of pepper to get relief from bad throat.

Skin

Banana is a natural skin whitener. Mash a ripe banana and apply it on the face and neck, and your tan colour will fade away.

Hiccups

Roast some peppercorns and breathe deeply. Your hiccups will stop at once.

Dysentery

A teaspoon of fenugreek seeds in a glass of lukewarm water will bring relief immediately.

Liver
To maintain your liver in a good condition, take a refrigerated pineapple slice dipped in honey, twice a day.

Hair
A mixture of almond oil, olive oil and castor oil in equal proportions acts as an excellent hair tonic.

Insects
(a) Place neem leaves in your books to prevent them from being attacked by insects.
(b) Burn neem leaves in the courtyard or garden to keep mosquitoes away.

Cold
Drink plenty of lime juice everyday as the ascorbic acid (Vitamin C) content of lime helps heal wounds quickly, maintain your teeth, helps also hair, nails and complexion in good condition and guard against catching colds.

Nose
Stop nose-bleeds by putting a few drops of pomegranate juice into your nostrils.

Lips
Massage your lips with coriander leaves juice for soft and rosy results.

Eyes
(a) Place cotton wool swabs dipped in cold milk on closed eyes to soothe the eye and remove dark circles.
(b) Triphalla (Amla+Harr+bahera) soaked in water overnight then boiled & filtered and to be applied to the eyes along with rose water.

Cough
If you are suffering from a nagging cough or chest congestion, boil three cups water with two fresh betal leaves & four crushed peppercorns, till the water is reduced to half. Strain and drink it every morning and night with a teaspoon of honey added to it.

Medicinal Value of Basil Leaves
(a) For immediate relief from toothache, take two basil leaves, a grain of salt and a pinch of pepper powder and press against the affected tooth.
(b) Mix equal quantities of basil juice, honey, and *ajwain* seed juice and drink on the empty stomach, if you are suffering from cough.

Tea
Tea is a wonderful drink. Brew your tea slowly, it takes three-

four minutes for the anti-oxidants to make their way into the water. Anti-oxidants delay ageing.

Motion Sickness

Chewing a couple of cloves while travelling will relieve motion sickness.

High B.P.

If you are suffering from high blood pressure, try this remedy. Boil two cups water with 10 to 15 basil leaves, a few peppercorns and a little sugar. Strain and drink it thrice a day.

Toothache

Take one teaspoon ginger juice, a little edible camphor, a little honey and a pinch of salt. Heat the mixture for a second and apply it on the aching tooth. You will get immediate relief.

Sore Throat

Powder peppercorns and basil leaves and dry them in the shade. Use this powder to make black tea.

Hair Loss

Dry lemon rinds, orange peels and pomogranate skin in the sun and grind to a fine powder. Mix this powder in coconut oil and apply to your hair to prevent hair loss and for glossy hair.

Acidity and Indigestion

Dry roast one teaspoon each of cumin seeds and *ajwain* seeds in a pan. Add one cup water and boil till it it reduced to half its quantity. Strain and add sugar to taste. Drink one teaspoon for relief from acidity and indigestion.

Nausea & Stomach Ailments

Take a slice of fresh ginger after each meal to protect yourself, from stomach ailments. For immediate relief from nausea, chew salted dry ginger sticks.

Stomach Upsets

For quick relief from an upset stomach, chew a spoonful of 'ajwain' (fennel seeds) with little black salt.

Cough, Nausea and Vomiting

Take half a cup of onion juice mixed with two teaspoons of honey for relief from cough, nausea & vomiting.

Toxicity

If mushrooms are poisonous, to check it, boil them in water along with a few garlic flakes. If water turns black they are poisonous.

Enuresis (Passing Urine at Night)

Chewing one teaspoonful of black sesame seeds (til) before going to bed cures enuresis.

Malnutrition

Banana is a complete food. It has all the ingredients necessary for body's nutrition, growth & strength. So, it is specially recommended for children and old people. But, it causes a little bit constipation so, it should be taken with black pepper & salt.

Habitual Abortion

Grind fresh flowers of Anar (2gms) to a fine paste. Add a little water and filter. Add sugar to taste in filtrate and use it morning and evening (taking 2gms flower each time) for three days.

Nausea/Bile

Sharbat of Imli cools liver/bile and checks nausea and vomiting especially in summer days. 5gms ripe fruit of *imli* dipped in water for 1/2 hours, after that, it is masticated in water and seeds are thrown out. Now, remaining water containing *imli* is taken in the afternoon with sugar.

Dropsy/Liver Inflammation

Leaves of Kasondi (1gm) and Kali mirch (7) is ground together in water and filtered. Take it morning and evening for one week (each time 1gm Kasondi & 7 Kali mirch).

For all kinds of Fever

Gilo (Gurach)-one gram is powdered form and dipped in water. Water is strained and divided in to two doses. Mix each dose with a spoon of sugar and take morning and evening. Better if Ajwain (250mg.) is also added to Gilo.

Face Cream

Chana ka atta (besan) ...	1/2 Cup
turmeric Powder ...	1 tsp
Mustard Oil ...	1/4 to 1/2 Cup

Mix all these materials to a semi-solid paste and apply it on your face. It will bring marvellous glow on your skin. It can be used on hands &legs also.

Cataract

Tobacco leaves ...	1 gram
Arandi ka Tel ...	4 grams

Mix these ingredients to a very fine paste and keep it in a small bottle. Apply it to eyes with a small rod daily.

Cough

White Pepper ...	1 gram
Mishri ...	250 mg

Grind these items to a very fine powder. Now, mix it with one tsp Malai and take it bit by bit rather lick it gradually.

Fever

Mix equal number of leaves of Basil, Neem and Lemon grass plus 7-10 black pepper. Boil it like, you make tea. Strain the water and drink 3/4 times a day to cure fever.

Gas/Giddiness

Dhania powder ... 1 gram
Khand ... 250 mg

Mix these two materials in the said ratio and keep it in a container, use a tsp after each meal with water.

Piles

While going to toilet, put a medium piece of Alum (Fitkari) in water. Use this water after the toilet. Repeat till relief.

Diarrhoea/Indigestion/Gas

Saunf and Dhania is to be mixed in equal proportion, powdered and a small amount of Mishri or Khand is added. 2 tsp is to be taken morning and evening. This will stop diarrhoea/indigestion / gas formation and is helpful to eyes.

Eye sight

One small piece of turmeric is kept in lemon and when it dries, turmeric is taken out & put in second fresh lemon and when it dries it is further kept in third/fourth lemon. Now,

turmeric is ground with one/two drops of water & applied on the eyes with the help of a rod for 7/10 days or as needed.

Cholera

Mix powdered red pepper with honey and prepare fine small pellets (equal to 1/2 pea size). Use 2 pellets when patient feels extreme weakness. It will bring dramatic relief in 2/3 days.

Dog-bite

In case of dog-bite, first apply mustard oil on that part and then pack it with red pepper powder. It will cure disease from spreading even if the dog is rabid.

Leprosy

Red Pepper (Powdered) ... 1 gm
Ghee ... 2.5 gms

Mix and keep it in a small container. Use it on the affected part twice or thrice a day. It will bring good results.

Abortion

Tender leaves of Babool ... 2 gms
Water ... 2 Cups

Boil it so that water becomes half. Strain, add *mishri* to taste. Use this 2/3 days once a day to check abortion.

Dandruff

Add a few drops of eucalyptus oil to the henna mixture before applying it on your hair if you want, dark copper colour. This also helps to get rid of dandruff and leaves your hair shining.

Toothache

For instant relief from severe toothache, press a little turmeric powder into the tooth.

High Blood Pressure

To control high blood pressure, mix equal quantities of onion juice and honey and take one teaspoon everyday in the morning.

Diarrhoea

(a) A strong cup of unsweetened black tea is effective in stopping diarrhoea.

(b) Another quick remedy is to peel apple and shred it. Keep the shredded pieces in a plate for approx 20 minutes until they turn brown in colour, and then eat them.

Constipation

Simply eat a few liquorice sticks to cure constipation.

Catarrh

To rid yourself of congestion, mix a teaspoon of vinegar in a glass of warm water and sip frequently.

Coughs

First cut an onion or several flakes of garlic into thin slices. Cover the slices with honey and leaves for two to three hours. Drink a spoonful of the resulting juice throughout the day.

Smelly Feet

Soak your feet in strong tea for 20 minutes everyday until smell disappears. To prepare your footbath, brew two tea bags in 500 ml of water for 15 minutes and pour the tea into a basin containing two litres of cool water.

Bleeding Gums

Take lemon juice in a glass of water daily for 3/4 days. Also gargle with salt. Sprinkle powdered turmeric and henna over the oozing blood. This will stop flow of blood immediately.

Chills

Instead of your regular hot tea or coffee, have a glass of hot water mixed with honey and lemon. Put a teaspoon of honey, lemon juice and a little grated ginger in a glass and add hot water stir and drink.

Cracked skin

Apply a mixture of grated potato soaked in olive oil. Leave this for 10 minutes and then rinse off.

Tired Eyes

Lavender oil offers gentle relief for tired for and strained

eyes. Add a drop of lavender oil to 500 ml of water & shake the solution well. Dip two cotton wool pads in the liquid, squeeze out the excess water and place one pad over each eyes (Don't use contact lenses at this time).

For General Debility

Sage is an excellent pick-me-up. Take 100gms of fresh sage leaves and soak them in a bottle of white wine for two weeks. Add honey for sweetening and leave for extra 24 hours. Use a muslin cloth for straining, making sure you press as you strain. Collect the solution in a bottle and drink a little before meal.

Spots

Herbs like tea tree oil and lavender oil, both antiseptics, can be applied neatly and quickly to pimples.

Warts

Place some chopped onions in a dish, cover with salt and leave overnight. Twice a day apply the resulting juice to the warts until they disappear.

Bad Breath

Chew some parsley leaves regularly remain your breath fresh. Alternatively, you can chew some cardamom seeds to sweeten your breath.

Indigestion

Place a teaspoon of freshly grated ginger into a pan and add

a cup of water. Cover and allow to simmer for five minutes. Strain the contents & drink.

Nausea

Powdered cinnamon and sliced ginger work by interrupting nausea signals sent from the stomach to the brain. If you are a herbal tea drinker, simply sprinkle powdered cinnamon on the tea and drink ginger tea to cure nausea.

Nose Bleeds

Dip a cotton bud in rose water and dab it on to the inside of your nostrils to stop the bleeding.

Bruises

Slice a raw onion and place over the bruise. But, do not apply this over grave injuries.

Toothache

Cloves are excellent painkillers. You can either chew one, or place it near the tooth. As the juices flow and mix with saliva, they numb the gum and alleviate pain.

Stomach Belches

Take a small piece of jaggery after eating radish to avoid unpleasant stomach belches.

Constipation

If you are often constipation, eat more of lady's finger.

Haemoglobin

Prepare leafy vegetable 'Sabji' in an iron 'Kadai'. It will taste good. The 'Kadai' is a good source of iron which is required to increase haemoglobin in blood.

Malaria

Taking one or two leaves or two of basil take care of many disorders and works wonders during malaria.

Sprain

Add a tsp of salt to two tsp turmeric powder and boil with a little water to obtain a thick paste. Apply while still hot over sprain.

Thirst

Take a cardamom or two especially during long journeys, to avoid feeling thirsty.

Nails

For glossy and strong nails, soak them in a mixture of lemon juice and glycerine.

To Check Bleeding

Sprinkle powdered turmeric and henna over the oozing blood. This will stop flow of blood immediately.

•••

IMMUNE SYSTEM AND ESSIAC

This formula works wonders for a depleted immune system, whatever disorder is the result of this depletion.

Essiac does three things: it cleans the blood, cleans the liver and oxygenates the cells. As a result of taking it, a sick person feels more energetic and has a greater sense of well-being.

Many romantic stories have grown up around the use of Essiac and numerous 'cures' are linked to it. I know personally many people who have benefited enormously from using it, and who have benefited enormously from using it, and who have baffled their doctors by overturning their prognoses.

INGREDIENTS

Burdock, root (*Arctium lappa*)
Sheep Sorrel, leaf (*Rumex acetosella*)
Slippery Elm, powder (*Ulvus fulma*)
Turkey Rhubarb, root powder (*Rheum officinale*)

The proportions of these 4 ingredients are in multiples of 4:

24 parts Burdock root
16 parts Sheep Sorrel
4 parts Slippery Elm
1 part Turkey Rhubard

METHOD

Add 100 gms/4 oz of the formula, in the above proportions of the 4 dried ingredients, to 5 litres/8 pt of spring water once the water has reached a rolling boil. Use a 10 litre/2-gallon vessel to boil this in for 12 minutes. Check that all the herbs are submerged in the liquid; replace the lid and leave the decoction to steep for a minimum of 6 hours (all night is ideal). Then, remove the lid again, and give it a good stir. Replace the lid and leave to steep for a further minimum of 6 hours.

Re-heat. Strain into sterile, hot bottles, label and use. The average shelf life is about a month.

DOSE

The dose is 4 tablespoonfuls diluted with an equal amount of boiling spring water. To be most effective, this dose should be taken on a fasting stomach - 2 hours before the dose without any food or drink and one hour after. For someone who is really ill, 3 doses a day may be taken-this is the maximum that should be taken. Try waking, taking the first dose and waiting one hour for

breakfast. Have lunch at, say, 1 p.m. You will have finished eating by 1.30 p.m., so eat or drink nothing until 3.30 p.m., when you take the second dose. Wait another hour and at 4.30 p.m. you can have tea, if you feel like it. When you have decided what time you want to go to bed, take no food or drink for 2 hours before that time, then take your last dose of the day and go to bed.

EFFECT OF TAKING ESSIAC

After 6 to 8 weeks of taking Essiac thrice a day, it will be possible to see distinct changes in your state of health. Some people find that changes happen quickly, others that they happen more slowly. Don't be either despondent or elated by this, because each person's system has its own pace. Minimising of pain can happen within 3-4 days of starting to take this formula.

Once you feel sure there has been an improvement, cut out the dose in the middle of the day and take 2 doses a day for the next 3-4 months. After that, you may feel, it is the right time to drop another dose. The evening dose may be the best one to retain, but you should make your own judgment, as you know your own body best. Stay on one dose a day for about 6 months. A maintenance dose of day twice a week can then be taken. Some people take this formula as a prophylactic, one dose a day from the beginning.

DECOCTION FOR GENERAL USE

INGREDIENTS

50 gms/2 oz Pot Barley (organic)
4 litre/5 pt spring water
2 oranges, or 2 lemons (organic, if possible)
100 gms/4 oz glucose powder

METHOD

Simmer the barley and water until the barley is soft and the water reduced by half. If the fruits are not organic, wash them first, then peel them carefully and chop the flesh into the liquid. If organic fruit is used, it can be washed and sliced straight into the liquid. Stir in the glucose powder until it is dissolved.

Allow the decoction to steep for about 12 hours - perhaps all night. Squeeze out the pieces of citrus fruit and discard the skins. Bottle the decoction and use it as soon as possible, while it is still fresh.

Lemon or orange or barley water is nourishing, soothing and refreshing, although the citrus in it may make it difficult to drink for people with mumps, measles, or chickenpox. If the sufferer doesn't like it, the curer can enjoy its qualities instead.

•••

GLOSSARY

Neem	–	Margosa
Mishri	–	Rock candy, large crystallized sugar
Gud	–	Jaggery
Ilaichi	–	Cardamom
Saunf	–	Fennel
Sonth	–	Ginger
Sag	–	Spinach
Malai	–	Cream